THE VALLEY OF SELF

Best Wishes
Maralee G Davis

maralee g. davis

For DAVID J. THIBAULT

(my husband)

who, perhaps, endured

more than I . . .

Printed in United States of America
Library of Congress Catalog number 78-91329
SBN # 87658-006-1

ACKNOWLEDGEMENTS

The Golden Quill Press - (XXXII) - Soliloquy's Virgin; Source of Book Title

Poetry Society of New Hampshire Newsletter

The Traveler (LIII & LVIII)

Flowers For A Neanderthal IV - Chapbook (LXIV)

National Federation of Poetry Societies - (American Mosaic prize winning poem - (XLI) - page 45)

Ballet On the Wind - Arizona State Poetry Society Anthology 1969 (LIX)

Golden Quill Press Anthology 1969

INDEX OF FIRST LINES

IN THE VALLEY

I

The giant
    is but a gentle self
Inside a cage
    like steel -
Late shed
    when self discovered truth
And soul
    did self-reveal.

II

At the grey of dawn
I am but a visitor
to my soul.
Gentle rain
feeding parched earth-lips
may impose its medley
to rouse me from slumber;
Or senses may alert
to the sensuous virgin snowfall –
death of autumn buried by new season;
Or redbreak of dawn – a season within seasons –
may force itself between the lids
of eye and mind;
But inevitably, sharp, exciting awareness
is shadowed with mysterious, lonely
wonderment
Of this infinitesimal spark of life – I –
that wanders deep-brief upon awakening
(beachcomber of self)
before coerced to the scurrying world.
No stranger,
but visitor still
to my lone soul.

III

Know yourself.
Know yourself
    and be free;
Be free of all pretense
    that chains you –
    victim of inner self.
What use the intellect,
    what use the hands,
    if you cannot be unshackled
    from forces that destroy?

IV

I do not want
    to conquer life
but drink
    from pools and springs –
drink all
    this thirsty soul requires
to understand,
    appreciate,
what hands –
    and God –
    create.

V

Night hours creep
on cricket–song
or winter's snowy whisper;
The heart knows years
within an hour –
a world extinct of human voice.

The desperate weaken
in crush of breath
While soul that harbors
hopeful ember
tears the self with salty tear –
Flesh is drained
of earthly strength
but mind is calmed in Godly sphere;

Emotion–dulled,
the ache subsides –
Yet eddys the endless cycle –
crescendo new exposes raw
serrated edge of longing.

VI

Emptiness – a hollow
bowl,
A waiting spoon to
feed,
Velvet soft, a robe
of red.
What meets the need
of need?

VII

Naked soul
    you agonize.
Can't the self
    recognize
No sublime persists?

Sublime! Sublime!
    What earthly hell
The struggling heart
    seeks to quell;
Yet faith exists.

VIII

I stood on the mountain
so tame
so wild –
Dared elements
to rape
unfeeling flesh;
Cold wind
I feel not
your bone scraping chill,
Wet rain
I feel not
your battering flood,
Hot sun
no sweat
do you draw
from my marrow.
I stood in the valley
so naked
so shaken –
Begged death repose
its rupturous wound,
Exclaimed love a traitor
with murderous heart
And time the worst beggar
and baker of bread.

(continued)

I stood by the sea
    and watched it absorb
    the wreckage of life –
    assume mask serene,
Its secrets
    well hidden;
It chanted to me
    'Come let me woo you –
    a lover I'll be.'
Yes, Lover,
    yes, Lover –
    a lover please be;
Taunt me
    and soothe me –
    rock me to sleep,
Pull me with tide
    to mysterious depth,
Let me but swim
    in the knowledge of self
And drown – finally drown –
    a whole person whole.

IX

Life moves
in sounds;
I walk.
Sun speaks
through chain link shadows,
clouds cross
The path
of footprints and voice prints.
Exploding motors,
And car radios
blanket bird chatter.
A clinking bike chain
As a boy passes
catches papers
and laughter
From a nearby print shop,
a fusing of sweat
and ink and lead.
Children shuffle
at hopskotch
happy in today.
Life moves
in sounds;
I walk –
Silent
and alone.

X

I stood on the shore
        and returned to my birth –
Horizon the scope
        of my soul.
Out of the waves
        splashed a gay, laughing child.
She played at the edge,
        unaware in her innocence,
Blissful, delighted,
        with world of the sea;
Shells and the seaweed
        and castles in sand.
The tide slithered in
        with strong undertow;
The child was divorced
        from her play –
Brief disappeared
        to emerge once again
As maiden
        with delicate form,
Soft smile
        in reserve of her eyes.
She lay on warm sand,
        sought rest from the struggle,
And slept
        in Apollo's embrace.
Perigee tide held her
        fast in its grasp;
I saw her swept back
        to the sea –
Soft trembling mouth
        silent remained
While eyes begged assistance
        she fought for control.

(continued)

I watched her return –
now woman was she –
With babe
at her breast.
She strode toward high ground
but on coral did stumble –
Each wave was a year
that lapped at her feet.
Child torn from her breast
gave a cry of distress.
Gentle did she
brush away sand,
Wipe tears from its face,
and kiss its soft cheek;
Then pushed it aside
toward the mountain of life.
Again I observed her
fight with the sea;
The waves closed about her –
ocean floor deathly near –
But her strength was renewed
by prayer.
My eyes saw her surface,
swim, touch the sand;
Unfaltering she walked
directly to me –
The gay, laughing child
I'd seen short before –
Recognition was instant
and *I was* once more.

ON THE MOUNTAIN

XI

Can one not measure love
By lack of things?
A fire without flame . . . the sea minus salt . . .
Crowns without kings . . .

XII

Share the earth –
but not the faces;
color them in background.
Love me whole,
as I love you,
and touch me – all –
with silent sound.
Granite be –
but tender ocean,
always change
yet fast devotion.
Place my grave
where next you'll be,
but let me go
first – selfishly.
No love that lives
can really die –
only sleeps
through by and by.
But till that sleep
let flesh and mind,
thoughts, emotions
intertwine.
Share the earth
and love me strong;
Exchange of love
is nature's song.

XIII

You come to me at night –
on wings of silence –
And sit upon my counterpane
laughing, whispering,
to the child I am again.

You come to me at night –
on wings of silence;
Holding counsel, you envelop me
with warm protection –
a friend I need steadfastly.

You come to me at night –
on wings of silence –
And touch me; lover – gentle, bold.
Soft caress, you possess –
heart and soul I full unfold.

You come to me at night –
on wings of silence;
Virile senses covet proof that you are near;
mind pretends while heart assures
you'll soon appear.

XIV

Wait for me at
summer –
meet me at the edge
of spring.
We'll touch the
valley's harvest
and with winter's sleep
I'll bring
the gentleness of
snow
upon autumn's
counterpane.

There'll be moods of
gale–whipped
meadow, naked
gentle rain
and rivulet
laughter
down twilight
country lane.
Should parting be in shroud
or sun –
Emotions' waves then
halcyon.

XV

It often hurts
        when one is led
down strange paths,
        and bled
is one when one
        can't find
the bee at work
        caressing flower. So blind
the heart that
        closes self –
dust that grows
        on empty shelf.
Trust the mind
        to grow with reason
but never turn
        from each love's season.

XVI

Dread of night . . .
volcanic silence . . .
this – your absence.
Vacant arms . . .
mind embraces . . .
this – your absence.
Hours build continents . . .
Alaskan winter . . .
this – your absence.
Child of Christmas . . .
Age of woman . . .
this your presence –
your return.

XVII

Welcome home,
    my darling,
with beautiful smile
    and hazel eyes.
Lost months –
    a continent of stone
(in rubble
    it now lies –
shattered
    under the sun).

XVIII

I glimpsed your
        naked soul –
and it was
        like mine.
I saw the ache
        you held –
the curtain you
        drew past –
the torment spiked
        and barrel-hooped
        about you.
The lonely stranger
        there
came out to shake
        his garments, brief,
and noticed I,
        chromatic fine,
        the sensitivity.
Stranger,
        so not hide
        yourself –
speak,
        speak in silence
        if you will –
        but speak.

(continued)

Remains the soul
as lone,
but life is
only worth
the mark
of sharing
carved upon
its face –
with sculptor's knife,
an implement
of love.

XIX

Choke not
        the perennial blossom, Love,
With greedy weeds – mistrust and doubt
        and ivys that poison.
No happiness was ever found
        in sumac beds –
        despite capacity for fruit and flower.
You say, 'never look back'
        but life revolves – point de repère.
Slash, cull, eliminate
        emotions' perversity.
Philanthropy of soul and heart
        creates palingenesis
        of spring and summer's intensity.
You'll find me in every blossom, Love;
Even blossoms sleep under the snow –
        or didn't you know?
        Or didn't you know?

XX

I knew a perfect moment
when water fell upon our nakedness
as we clasped each other
And we were washed
to childhood innocence
in our moment of revelation.
God touched the silver drops
that slid down grateful faces
and travelled down white bodies
to a new awareness.
Your voice – sifted from the jungle –
was the greatest gift
my ears received.
Your eyes – pools of long starvation –
knew plenty in that perfect moment,
which fed by mine, bared the soul.
My own long drought was over
and the universe
became so infinitesimal
that my heart contained it all.
I knew a perfect moment,
when the agony was gone –
as two minds burst ovule to blossom –
and God painted us as one . . .
painted us as one
for that one perfect moment.

XXI

You sleep.
Though you sleep we are married.
Marriage, I once thought,
Was all the waking, loving, doing things –
But it is also sleep.
It is sleep
With your breath soft across my face,
A gentle snore –
Responsibility momentarily lifted,
The power of brain and muscles relaxed.
It is a turning toward me –
Eyelids half aroused
In quest to fling your arm about me.
It is a turning away
Yet an outflung leg seeking
To touch my toes with yours –
Caressingly, reassuringly.
It is the clean, sensuous smell of your flesh;
I move close against you,
My arm reaching about you –
Your arm locks mine
Hard against your chest
With soft hair and velvet skin
Stretched taut across your ribcage;
Resumes the gentle snore –
My face pressed against the cool flesh of your back,
My breathing slows, mates the rhythm of your body;
I listen to that gentle snore –
The world forced to half its pace as you sleep.
You sleep . . .
And though you sleep we are married.

IN THE FOREST

XXII

'Lonesome' ravenously bites in greedy chunks;
        the gaping hole bleeds,
And scarlet sluice drapes down mute Greek statues;
        no flowers blossom
        no warm winds blow –
        only the stenching agonies of alone–alone.

XXIII

When you turn your back
    I am the eye of a needle –
    hollow, empty.
I have much to offer
    but without you
    I have nothing to give.
You are the thread which binds
    the seam of life
    to life.
You are my husband;
    I am
    your wife.

XXIV

You turn me inside out –
    acid splashed on soul.
Whisper–soft you love me,
    bleed me; hunter's knife
    claims toll.
You draw me close –
    to disappear, crystal ball,
    self–centered sphere.

XXV

Scatter the crumbs
        that I may survive
Till the season
        of plenty.
Winter snows drift
        around corners of heart;
You watch - while I
        ache, shiver -
And feed me half-smile
        instead of embrace.
With quick winter
        thaw
You glow flame
        of fire,
Then you withdraw -
Distant reflection
        glazes your eyes.
Kaleidoscoped past
        scrapes your mind raw;
Countenance freezes
        and stranger appears -
The stranger knows not
        why inner self weeps
Or that weeping
        is he.
But the sleeping self knows
        deep hidden reason
Why arms stretch
        in slumber
Towards one
        who eats crumbs.

XXVI

When spirit, passions, starve
    the mind begins to crack
Like spider webs of brittle china,
    and white is edged with black.
Arms of understanding,
    a soft, firm voice of care
Checkmates inner chaos
    and binds the ugly tear.

A woman's strength is not her own –
    its substance comes from man
As did his rib, her counterpart;
    his tender touch she needs command.
Fast life ebbs when first he fails
    to gift her of his strength,
And sad her world – her bountiful world –
    when cut to black in length.

XXVII

I do not belong here –
      another life waits.
Reality is chains,
      chains around the moon,
A vast jug of sunshine,
      the jug tightly sealed.
In my world there's dancing
      and very much love –
Fantasia . . . Fantasia . . .
No one can barter,
      no evil takes root,
A smile opens doors
      and the heart has a home.
I do not belong here,
      your life is pretense;
Your humans are ice factories
      with bowels of coin,
Meters for faces
      with gluttonous smiles.
My world is filled
      with apricot dawn,
Purple of Concord
      and ribbon of sea.
Your world is full
      of transparent bodies,
Gears for their hearts,
      clocks for their souls.
Fantasia . . . Fantasia . . .
      oh to behold
A love to match mine.

XXVIII

Drink, you Merchants,
drain every vessel of blood;
Squeeze every ounce
of love from the soul.
Drink, you Merchants
feast and partake
Every offering of self
each human has made.
Obese Merchants,
pick at your teeth,
Get drunk –
drunk from your reign of power
For down on your knees
you'll once again pray –
Forgiveness –
for raping the flower.

XXIX

Death, Death –
    blissful sleep;
No more searing
    tears to weep,
No bitter words
    upon the ear –
Words that coil
    around heart, gash
    inner sphere
Choking,
    flesh and mind.
Death, Death –
    merciful, kind.

XXX

I hit the ocean floor
when I slashed my wrist.
(He said he'd never loved me;
and I had no one.)
It was a long, dark night.
Morning came
and I forgave him
because he loved me.
Next time –
if there must be a next time –
I shall not slash my wrist;
I shall merely close my eyes
and die.

XXXI

Naked,
We tore at each other's breasts
To grasp the hearts within;
Claws raked deep
and fences grew
Until he stood rebellious
in final declaration.
He raped my strength.

Emotions drained,
I touched thin blade
to warm flesh sensitive,
and pressure–soft, a red line drew.
No.
I could yet feel this flesh.
Yes.
The words cut more –
But were not true.
No more than I
Could he turn
on all we'd borne
In laughter
and canyon silence.
No,
his words were mulled in wine.
I feasted silence –
which built a century –
To hear those words wiped clean.
Two words –
'I'm leaving.'
Two –
and with them left
the sense of touch.
I would not hear him –

(continued)

I would not hear him say there was no love.
Yet false words reached my ears
      and sound was magnitudinous –
      while touch was small.
A throbbing pulse – his words –
      and flesh turned numb.
He moved to leave . . .
      and quick across the wrist
      I slashed a deeper line.
The sting was *sweet*
      across my mind –
      the body cold, deliberate.
So leave me, so leave me;
      but you shall not leave me –
      not without knowledge
      of how I love you.
Rich blood, healthy blood,
      down the skin,
      down the drain.
NOW say 'I do not love you.'
Say those words again!
Purged, the blood; the barrier fell –
      cleansed, the naked soul.
He sang to me; and naked we stood.
And naked we stood – but together.

XXXII

You've won! You've won!

Your barbed wire fence
    was strung too well;

Your fortress wall
    was too well laid.

No more strength
    have I, to scale

Its rocky heights
    against the winds.

You've won! You've won!
My armour rusts.

The lamp I held
    you shattered first.

My boots have great
    and gaping holes.

My feet are mud;
    I cannot run.

You've won! You've won!

XXXIII

The gates
        once open wide
Are trapped –
        arabesque –
        in rust.
Unclothes, the voice;
        yet untouched
        by washing ripples
        of spring
Where redbreak of dawn
        once flamed.
No violets pierce
        the core benumbed;
Once valiant heart
        now fearful trembles
Corrosion pits
        too deep the dust.

XXXIV

So goodbye . . . so goodbye . . .
to love unawakened;
The drought
has stripped
And wrest
its toll.
Passioned thought,
gentle embrace,
And rainbow emotion
lie buried on the knoll
Of autumn.
How well you managed
To eclipse
the sun's warmth
With indifference –
the turning away;
Spare
you rationed time
And gave of yourself.
You do not know how to love,
my love,
So blame you,
I cannot,
For having thieved
all sweet, precious moments
You could not know exist.
Thus,
You cannot know . . . you cannot know . . .
I love you so,
my husband, my husband.

XXXV

Your kiss is now like Christmas snow
on a quiet night when
clamoring streets are empty
and streetlights split the darkness
Exposing the white carpet and the glistening
Baptismal flakes.
It was once like warm spring rain and
the first fragrant violet - your kiss.
And with the passing of that tender season,
I knew its summer warmth and passion
of nakedness in the hot sun
and salty breakers of the sea. I knew
the splendor of Autumn - with your kiss -
the colors so precisely matching
those of my heart and soul.
Now falls the snow - and I mourn
for Christmas shall pass and with it the snow
and the streetlight will go out
exposing the black empty street -
and the death of a kiss . . .
the death of a kiss . . .

XXXVI

You closed a door, my Love,
          and with that gesture
          the 'self' accordioned to childhood;
A traumatic drought relived,
          scavenged bones of the soul -
          if a soul has a skeleton.
One little door - too much
          a barrier, Love -
and you have lost a precious
          part of me.
Precisely which part and how much
          this moment does not know
but the barrier is marble. You could not
          reach me now. Cold away
you held me - indifferent
          to needs the fire. Why breathe
on yesterday's ashes - the hearth
          lies empty, devoid of warmth;
Your own neglect, my Love,
          your own neglect.

XXXVII

Dust is my destiny;
Though I crumble
                before you
And stalk
                the skyline in loneliness
I have yet to crash
                the cover on ignorance,
Yet
                the sparrow to be,
Yet
                the mountain to burn,
Yet
                to lie on temptress' bed.
Barefooted I rise
                clothed only
                in wistfulness.
Dust is my destiny –
Despite the yearning
                you'd want me more.

XXXVIII

I allow a path
    and underground memories
burst alive.
    It is almost too much –
the ache
    that splices yesterday
and
    today.
Like the sharp line –
    (equator
between sanity
    and insanity)
passion –
    not to be torn free,
clutches
    like hot taffy
virgin to shape
    or mold.
The sonic clock
    shatters the path
and I am left
    with spacious reality;
You are gone . . .
    you are gone . . .
Poignant ghost –
    torturous ghost –
Beloved sprite
Of my island
    past.

XXXIX

The sea is sooner calmed
than the heart that aches;
The sea never calms
in the heart that breaks.

XL

Island sentinel –
    the vacant old house;
Victorian monument
    with empty eyes
(Mesmerized, they stare
    at the sea).
Claim me! Claim me!
    Make me live
    or let me die.
Let someone care!
    Let someone care!
    Or wind and waves
    destroy me now –
Why prolong
    the agony?
But a memory –
    children's laughter,
(Happy feet
    upon the stairs),
Family chatter
    midst warm activity,
Kitchen cookery
    whetting appetites,
Emblazoned bodies
    (sun kissed,
    sea and moon drenched);
Claim me, someone!
    Claim me!
Open wide my portals
    to human sound –
    lovers' embrace.
Give purpose
    to my structure;
Give me life
    or gift me to the sea.

XLI

One grain of sand
added to another –
Needs the oyster –
produces the pearl,
and nourishes
man's brother.

One grain of thought
added to another
Feeds the soul –
creates a gem –
breathes life
into man's brother.

One grain of love
added to another
Seeds the heart,
unfolds the gift –
the universe
for man's brother.

XLII

The tide of time has washed me to you –
The surf is my laughter; the spray,
my tears;
White caps – spontaneous – affection
appears
for you to catch glimpse of;
bayadere
of emotions and colours am I.
Will you paint me? Will you love me
by and by?
Will you haunt me, will you taunt me,
make the heart cry
if you're not near?
Even now it slight
depends
on your thoughts expressed in kaleidoscope.
Wend
your way to me – if but brief, a
moment share
the beauty of the white caps; to
salty surf be heir.

XLIII

The seagull tried strange food
        and found itself
        a friend
that disappeared. Who's to say
        another might not be around
        the bend
of rock to sea to toss
        the gull
        still another
delicacy? And is it better
        that he try it,
        while his brother
watches only, or is he wrong
        to taste what whets
        his appetite
for unknown things, to taunt
        his senses that
        may not quite
ever be fulfilled?

XLIV

You gave me bread
and washed my wounds
with wine of care.
In my hands
I held a sunset
tangerine –
Laced by sea,
Urania blue,
Veronese green.
This I offered –
palms outstretched –
in return,
With soul
of boundless
limitation.
Verity . . .
reality . . .
For what purpose
did you will me
life?

XLV

I cannot love you
    as I loved before –
Too much has
    come between;
But love once held
    in ocean waves
Leaves salty spray
    that clings
As little pools
    in rocky niches –
Little pools that
    gleam
When sunshine warms
    with gentle touch,
Little pools that
constant yearn
For parent-sea's
    trenchant clutch.

XLVI

Sandpiper lonely –
    scavenging shore –
Restless the waves;
    shiny the lure,
White–splashed old salt.
Wind is the season –
    tears from the clouds –
Sandpiper lonely;
    love is the fault.

XLVII

A lake and the sea
    once storm–wise
    met.
The sea returned,
    the lake grew calm,
    and neither claimed
    regret.

XLVIII

I have not laughed
    since last we laughed –
Nor felt the sun
    upon my breasts.
The ocean's mist
    has left my face;
I can no longer
    touch the stars.
Revolves – the axis –
    Still I'm apart
Standing lone,
    bewildered, lost.
My mind knows how
    we reached for life,
Where we met,
    and what we shared;
The richest gravestone
    to be laid
Marks the memory
    of HOW WE CARED.

XLIX

The edge of depths –
thus by the sea –
Where Christmas never changes,
where the soul sings
free
Of crowded thoughts
and thoroughfares,
and serenity prevails.
God give me strength
to greet the challenge
of frigid faces –
apathists –
needful of warmth.
Kindle my fires
that I may burn
the embittered shell
from frightened passersby.
Give me the gift
of sun and sea
so I may drown
in Christmas giving.

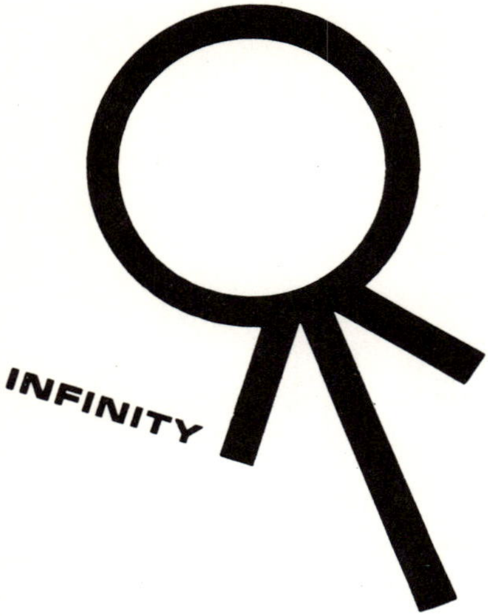

L

The way I live
is my own
conscience;
Neither masked
nor of any
consequence.

LI

Extremes of life might seem to be
    oft volcanic constancy,
Yet nature sleeps while pulse
    throbs blood.
(Rio Grande – warm, serene;
    deathly flood.
New England – quiet, cold;
    chisel down, her nature's gold.)
Earthly moods, human emotion –
    much the same – infinite sky,
    depth of ocean;
Cycle old repeats anew,
    hope and faith – love comes, too.
But never changes – gentle heart –
Where Christmas lives each day in part.

LII

No tree bore more abundant beauty –
in the spring of its decay.
The workers laboured for their queen
and kissed each fragrant blossom
While ivory mass hugged gnarled old limbs
and daybreak smelled of life and love.
Cloudburst brought the rain to beat
the petals from its breast;
Fruit of green then burst with life
as each limb strained to nuture child;
But struggle lost to summer drought –
the leaves were burned and apples fell.
Premature, its naked limbs
await the shroud of winter.
Perhaps once more the old tree's veins
will suck spring air – to bleed –
And lure the bees toward love affair
with its remaining blossoms.
I could not strike the sharpened axe
against this sturdy heart –
The proper funeral, then, must be
the time of nature's choosing.

LIII

Beat on, oh clock,
let farmer rise
to milk his cows
And laughing children
climb the bus –
with castle dreams
and knightly fears.
Let the drudge
be on with work,
and fatten
hypochondriac.
Rouse the meek –
inherit, they,
beauty
out of ugliness.
Judgement pass
upon the shrew
and wake the wicked
from his apathy.
Tell the bored
he'll go to hell
unless he'll rise
and work with you.
Beat, oh time,
you cradle all –
the rise of magnate,
and prostitute–call.
Like King of Beasts
supreme you reign –
the aging chronic,
the youthful dream.
Beat on, oh clock –
rake human tears –
but fall you must

(continued)

to aspen knee
Before the god
created pulse;
No rest, no rest –
emancipation –
Mere slave remain
to all creation.

LIV

Empty estates – the aging lone
    stripped to velvet bone,
Hollow of purpose, love vacated,
    transparent voice–prints
Unheralded.
Sad, the unloved,
    passing as night,
Unseen, unheard, untouched;
No rocket goals nor virile spring
    eyes downcast
That meet
    the shuffle of tired shoes
Not yet devoid of flesh.

LV

Into the land of castles you conceived me –
    midst champagne glitter and
    pre–depression spoils.
Baby food, strained by the hand of a maid,
    was my diet – alternated with fairy tales
    by baby sitters and pets that kept dying.
Space was my dessert –
    I've kept scrapbooks of memory –
    I tasted the frosting of aircraft
    tossed among clouds
    and drank the frappe
    of a fishing tug
    (my tiny hands on its wheel).
You showed me how wood and stone molded
    fortresses to hide a man and wife
    from prying eyes of an unloving world.
You brought me a nugget of fool's gold
    from a mountain in Colorado –
    where the family silver was mined.
You showed me how to plant a flower;
    you dressed me well; and once stood me
    in front of my grandmother's radiant harp.
You were good to me – in the time you gave me –
    but you gave me too much for a child of six;
A simple love would have sufficed –
    or if you had but listened – just once –
    to the music in my heart
And recognized
    the ocean of poetry there.

LVI

Despairing child
on ward cot lay,
dully stared in space –
So much, so much,
oh, God, so much,
she so longed to erase;
Screeching addicts,
sloe–eyed whores,
vulgar bitches
with drunken snores,
Vomit retched
against the wall,
urine stench –
blood and all,
Brazen roaches
chewing crumbs
from clothes encrusted
with human waste,
Tasteless food,
restraining bars,
all defunct
of kindly face.
Would no one claim her?
Would no one claim her?
Forgive abortion,
attempt on life;
Incentive give –
a will to live –
restore the beauty,
free inner strife?
She could not paint,
she could not paint,
what others so dictated.
She *must* be free –
She *must* be free –

(continued)

develop this, in trust.
Creative burden,
hands with gift,
jiva soul.
So much to lift
Beyond the fringe
of yesterday –
and today,
and today.
She looked about
infested room,
excreting rats
and bodies strewn
By willful choice
upon the floor,
and pledged her God,
"No more! No more!"
She'd rise again,
she'd rise again,
take life at truest length;
She'd found a key,
beneath all depth,
to bare a vault of strength.
Teen child stood tall
midst groaning flesh
and viewed inhuman sea,
And feeling life
with redbreak edge –
grew
a woman free.

LVII

He was a stranger –
    at the cemetery
    where relatives stood
    to commit his body
    to rest.
I thought of lilacs
    and apple blossoms
    and wondered
    what this man –
    who died alone –
    had been.
My granduncle, they said,
    but that is all
    I knew.
They failed to mention
    how he laughed
    or what gnarled hands,
    once young, had done
    to shape the world
    about him.
Relieved they were –
    with family pride –
    that he should die
    with cash enough
    to buy a decent burial.
No one wept –
    or really mourned
    this old man's death.
But I, a stranger,
    too,
    took Bible words
    from the mouth
    of the minister
And gently laid them

(continued)

before the body --
blessed with meaning
from the depth
of my heart -
And wished his soul
Godspeed
to the heavens.

LVIII

My shadow is young,
    my nude form exquisite;
My body is bronzed
    by the sun of your smile,
    the rays of your love.
I dance to fantasia,
    am supple of limb,
    ecstatic of heart.
I sing with the wind -
    zephyr to gale,
Wear spring in my hair
    and nails painted blue.
My mirror is gold,
    oval, ornate -
    stark fragment of truth
Where soft autumn face
    wistfully reflects.

LIX

Night River –
    you carry your secrets well.
What loves have touched the edges
    of your restlessness?
Whose sun–laughter did you share?
Where are they now
    who saw the hills burn their splendor?
Did they race against crisp, brown leaves
    and catch a breath of frosted dawn?
Where now are those loves?
Did they disappear to warmth of home
    or vanish with instant of hurricane?
Was moon–harvest an end, or a beginning?
You heard them whisper –
    secrets well collaged in your raven depth
Flowing endlessly; you carry them as puppets
    swept to sea . . .
Puppets of tumbling sun and spilling discontent . . .
You guard them well, Night River;
    those voices lost in sheltered mystery.

LX

I loved a child
    that was a stranger.
But momentary
    was our meeting;
A lad of four
    with tattered shirt
But clean of face
    with soulful eyes.
He turned to me
    amid the crowd
    of busy, frigid men,
Looked long
    and longing.
I smiled
    and spoke to him;
Trivial words
    but full of voice
    and desire to give.
I could not turn away from him.
    He drank me in
    with eyes unwavering,
    drank hard and long –
    to last an eon.
This child is starving . . .
    This child is starving . . .
I sought to give him
    one full moment.
Reaching out
    I touched his head –
    no parent could feel more.
"You're a good boy," I said,
    and with those words
    tried to tell him
    love would find him –

(continued)

love can come from strangers.
I loved this child
that was a stranger . . .
I loved this child
that remained a stranger . . .

LXI

Inside the drawer an empty locket lies
        untouched by dust of generations.
Once it held a lover's face –
        montage of moments long erased.
Sheltered in its darkened niche,
        forgotten . . . unclaimed . . . unwanted,
This precious piece, so wasted,
        contains the nectar of love once tasted.

LXII

(Tannenbaum)

GREEN, on white and under blue,
        fervent incense - life your own -
Sentinel with needled bough
        bared to wind and sleet,
Summer's parching sun;
        year by year to stretch
Your tearful core
        waiting, waiting for your purpose.

Guardian of rivulet? Fawn?
        Lovers' confidence held secret?
Shelter for the hunted -
        and the huntress?
Sliver impaled in heart
        of alcazar?
Or are you destined
        to metal cuneiform
Assaulting your skeleton -
        exposing sap
At the feet of children
        enchanted with Christmas;
A nimbus moment - short lived -
        but nonetheless
Preponderate
        in the scheme of things?

Whatsoever your mission,
        GREEN, on white and under blue,
I salute you and lionize your purpose.

LXIII

Would that Christmas dawn
in hearts of men
who never felt its grasp,
Nor heard the voice of child
ecstatic at its task
Of scarlet ribbon
around tissue white –
or emerald all encompassing
the thoughtful gesture.
Would that bitter men
breathe down to soul
and lungs near burst –
compassion –
While flakes of snow
disguise their tears
of new and gentle fashion.
Would that Christmas essence
reach new depths
and thanks for friendships
evoke a prayer
To crack the shell
to bare the pit
of vibrant understanding.
And may these men
see past the tinsel,
the rainbow baubles,
the yule log glow,
And know the reason
for the star.
And may these men
but dare allow
the gift of love
to open shallow lives.

LXIV

(WHAT 'MOOR' – NEANDERTHAL IV?)

Neanderthal Man –
untouched by intangible demand?
Unscathed by pressures
that vise the self?
Did he dream
of imaginary worlds to come –
And come they did – or, was his
the narrow path of mind, of living?
And was he giving?
Fragments of past bear witness –
Someone cared –
heaped his bier
bright of wildflowers.
Could Neanderthal Man and Neanderthal Woman
have laughed
and cried
Over a Neanderthal Child,
and dreamed
and worried,
Before Neanderthal Man died?
Bodies decay,
dreams may sleep,
caves build secrets,
nations weep –
The cycle unending;
Neanderthal Man's reach
extends the simple spheres;
What distance
is 60,000 years?